# VALDIS GRENKOVS

TRANSLATED BY ULDIS BALODIS
AND KATE WAKELING

A modern nursery rhyme from Latvia #006

# NAUGHTY GNAT

ILLUSTRATOR
ZANE ZLEMEŠA

# JIMMY DRAWS A PATH

## AND NEXT TO IT A FIELD OF BLOOMS

IS TIP-TOP.

DRAT. WHEREVER SHE PLAYS HER FOOTPRINTS STAY.

— OH, WHAT A TO-DO!

First published in the UK in 2018 by the Emma Press, Birmingham
Originally published in 2015 as "Negantā muša" by Liels un mazs, Riga, Latvia

Text © Valdis Grenkovs, 1959
English-language translation © Uldis Balodis and Kate Wakeling, 2018
Illustrations © Zane Zlemeša, 2015

**BICKI-BOOKS**
Artistic director – Rūta Briede
Design – Rūta Briede and Artis Briedis

Printed in Latvia by *Talsu tipogrāfijā*
on *Munken Print Cream* 115 gsm and *Carta Integra* 265 gsm

A CIP catalogue record of this book is available
from the British Library
All rights reserved.

ISBN 978-1-910139-98-1
theemmapress.com

Supported by Latvian Writers' Union
(*Latvijas Rakstnieku Savienība*) and
Ministry of Culture of the Republic of Latvia